Original title:
I Am More Than a Daydream

Copyright © 2024 Book Fairy Publishing
All rights reserved.

Editor: Theodor Taimla
Author: Melani Helimets
ISBN HARDBACK: 978-9916-759-14-1
ISBN PAPERBACK: 978-9916-759-15-8

Dreams With Substance

In the quiet night, where stars do gleam,
Visions rise, like tides in dream.
Hopes and fears, entwined they dance,
Guided by the moon's soft glance.

In shadowed realms, futures mold,
Stories whispered, brave and bold.
Heartbeats echo, silent calls,
Within these dreams, our spirit sprawls.

Mountains high and rivers deep,
Journeys start when we are asleep.
Paths unknown, yet clearly seen,
In the heart of each night's queen.

As dawn's light begins to clear,
Dreams with substance still adhere.
Guiding us through waking hours,
With the strength of unseen powers.

Keep those visions close, yet free,
Whispers of what we can be.
In the daylight, take their lead,
Dreams with substance are our creed.

Beyond the Glass

A windowpane of fragile dreams,
Reflects the light of morning beams.
The world outside, a vibrant hue,
Beyond the glass, a life anew.

Shadows dance on golden fields,
A canvas where the heart can yield.
Whispers of the wind, they pass,
In tales untold, beyond the glass.

Mountains rise where skies embrace,
Rivers flow in endless grace.
From here to there, in moments fast,
We glimpse the world beyond the glass.

Silent nights of starry bliss,
Hold promises of what we miss.
The moonlit paths where lovers pass,
Unveil the dawn, beyond the glass.

Reality's Tapestry

Threads of life in colors bright,
Weave a story through the night.
Every stitch, a memory,
In reality's vast tapestry.

Moments fleeting, yet they bind,
A fabric rich with heart and mind.
Textures smooth and moments free,
In the dance of life's decree.

Dreams and fears in woven strands,
Hold the world within our hands.
Through the warp and weft they flee,
Crafting shared reality.

Time, the weaver, ever true,
Binding red and gold and blue.
Patterns born of destiny,
In the loom of who we be.

In the Flesh of Fantasies

Whispers of a distant land,
Drawn by an invisible hand.
In the merest sigh or breeze,
Lies the flesh of fantasies.

Castles built on clouds above,
Guarded by the dawn of love.
Mermaids sing in silver seas,
Echoes in our reveries.

Romance blooms in desert sands,
Held by time's untethered strands.
Every dream a starry tease,
In the flesh of fantasies.

Masks and mirrors hold our gaze,
Twisting nights in playful maze.
In the fabric of these sprees,
Lies the flesh of fantasies.

Tangibility of Dreams

From midnight thoughts, dreams take flight,
In the silence of the night.
Visions dance with moonlit gleams,
In the tangibility of dreams.

Footsteps trace the paths unknown,
Journeys where the soul has flown.
Through the veil of twilight seams,
Lies the tangibility of dreams.

Stars align in perfect chance,
In this wondrous, fleeting dance.
Living in the golden beams,
Of the tangibility of dreams.

Waking hours feel so pale,
Compared to this ethereal tale.
Yet reality reclaims its themes,
From the tangibility of dreams.

Cotton Candy Realities

Pastel dreams in twilight skies
Whispers weave where silence lies
Moments dance on whimsy's tread
In realms where everyday is fed

Clouds of sugar, spun and bright
Colors melt in morning light
Truths dissolve in candied air
Hopes and wishes, ever fair

Seasons blend their fleeting hues
Magic found in daily views
Touch the sky with gentle hand
Feel the pulse of fairyland

Echoes drift in syruped streams
Life, enmeshed in softer dreams
Cotton worlds that drift and gleam
Bringing solace to extreme

The World behind the Daydream

Beyond the veil of waking thought
Lies a realm where dreams are caught
Chasing whispers, shadows bend
Lost in fancies without end

Meadows blooming, colors rare
Skies alight with gentle flair
Every thought, a flowering tree
Bearing fruit of reverie

Footfalls light on lands unknown
Mysteries in twilight shown
Wanderlust in silent sprees
Mapping out our secret seas

Eyes aloft, the mind takes flight
Dancing with the stars at night
Worlds unveiled when clouds disperse
Finding truth in dreamt converse

Audible Silhouettes

Notes that echo through the air
Silhouettes of sound laid bare
Songs that shape the unseen thread
Woven from the words unsaid

Melodies that softly rise
Painting shadows in the skies
Harmonies that blend and weave
Stories sung you won't believe

Rhythms pulsing in the dark
Tracing lines where passions spark
Every beat a whispered tale
Written in the moonlight's trail

Voices drift on breezes thin
Captured in the mourner's hymn
Audible, the shapes they form
Symphonies in silence born

Breathing Between Fantasies

In the spaces dreams unfold
Breath of life in stardust mold
Moments caught in twilight's seam
Dancing on the edge of dream

Whispers speak in windswept tones
Secrets hidden in heart's zones
Glimpses of the yet-to-be
Painted in our reverie

Breaths inhaled in mystic lore
Exhaled whispers, ever more
Threads of thought that intertwine
Fantasies that feel divine

In the silence thoughts ignite
Breathing in the endless night
Worlds anew with each inhale
Fantasies on which we sail

Flowing into Reality

Dreams like rivers fast engage,
In the currents change and swell,
Whispers soft on every stage,
In their depths do secrets dwell.

Imagination blends with night,
Casting shades on waking's sigh,
Through the mist, a glimmered light,
Turns to stars in morning's sky.

Fragments sharp of thoughts unwind,
Crafting worlds with painted hue,
In the pulse of time confined,
Truths from fancies born anew.

Hopes in Flesh

Mortal coils that strive to soar,
Binding futures to the bone,
Dreams entwined with sinew core,
Flesh and soul in hearts are sewn.

Longing pulses firm and strong,
In the veins of human plight,
Crafted stories, ancient song,
In each wish for morning light.

Hopeless times and trial's fire,
Shape the will with iron frame,
Hopes in flesh that never tire,
Burning bright in life's acclaim.

Grit and Grace

In the midst of troubled day,
Carved from stone, resilience beams,
Paths with grit we do not sway,
Guided by our fervent dreams.

Grace descends like morning dew,
To the weary and the lost,
Grit and grace, both tried and true,
Hold together, none exhaust.

Strength entwined with gentle patience,
Moulds our hearts through strife's embrace,
Bound in life's relentless cadence,
Facing fate with grit and grace.

Materialized Whimsy

Whims of fancy take their flight,
Weave the air with colors bright,
In the realms of fragile night,
Dreams are born in shadowed light.

Ideas dance on edges fine,
Crafted from a fleeting thought,
In the flicker hearts align,
Magic from the chaos wrought.

Substance from the ether springs,
Shapes of wonder, whims made real,
Wings of whimsy, soaring things,
Turn the abstract to the feel.

Whispers of Reality

In night's embrace, where silence speaks,
Reality whispers, softly weeps.
Shadows dance on moonlit beams,
Haunting truths in fractured dreams.

Stars weave tales of distant past,
Fairy light that will not last.
Truths unveiled in morning's light,
Vanished wishes out of sight.

Misty morn, the dawn of day,
Waking worlds in disarray.
Echoes from the twilight's song,
Reveal the places we belong.

In the quiet of our minds,
Secrets hidden, truth that binds.
Whispers of the world we see,
Reflections of reality.

Lives unfold, in patterned ways,
Endless nights and boundless days.
Yet, in whispers soft and low,
Reality's voice will always show.

Beyond Fleeting Fantasies

Through the veil of fleeting dreams,
Beyond the world's discordant screams.
Lies a realm where hearts are free,
In the space of fantasy.

Colors blend in vibrant hue,
Skies of gold and seas of blue.
In this world, so wild, so grand,
Magic woven through the land.

Here, the time does not constrain,
Moments held in sweet refrain.
Wanderers of this mystic shore,
Find a life they seek for more.

Beyond the grasp of fleeting thought,
Treasures held that can't be bought.
In this realm of endless flight,
Fantastical beyond the night.

Yet as dawn begins to rise,
Dreams dissolve before our eyes.
Leaving echoes pure and bright,
Of a world in fantasy's light.

Echoes in the Sunlight

Morning breaks with golden rays,
Sunlight dances, skies ablaze.
Echoes of a night's repose,
In the dawn, the world arose.

Whispers of the birds' sweet song,
Threads of light so clear, so strong.
Mirrored in the dew-kissed morn,
Life anew is softly born.

Footsteps on the tender grass,
Moments that we yearn to grasp.
Time's own echoes, fleeting, bright,
Captured in the morning light.

Nature's voice, a gentle breeze,
Rustling through the ancient trees.
Silent words that touch the soul,
In the sunlight, we are whole.

Day unfolds, its stories told,
Within its golden grasp to hold.
Echoes linger, fade from sight,
Yet remain in sunlight's light.

In the Wake of Visions

Dreams arise, in night's embrace,
Visions form and interlace.
Woven threads of future's past,
In their wake, some truths will last.

Eyes are closed, yet sight remains,
Boundless thoughts that break the chains.
In the quiet, worlds unfold,
Mysteries and myths retold.

Shadows lift, and light reveals,
Fractured whispers, time that heals.
In the wake of visions clear,
Paths of hope and roads of fear.

Through the dark, and into dawn,
Where the light of day is drawn.
Visions fade, but still they guide,
Silent strength, deep inside.

Wisdom found in silent nights,
Leads us through our daily plights.
In the wake of visions true,
Futures bright we dare pursue.

Colors of Substance

In spectrum's glow we seek the real,
Hues that touch, and tones that feel.
From red's deep flame to blue's cool guise,
Truths in color grace the skies.

Yellow whispers of the dawn,
Green of life, and dew on lawn.
Purple shadows, secrets keep,
While white in purity does sleep.

Orange dances, warmth alive,
Black in solemn night's derive.
Brown of earth, so rich, so kind,
Each with stories intertwined.

Gray in mystery resides,
Where every shade and tint collides.
Colors blend, and through the art,
Find the essence of the heart.

Tangible Nightmares

Shadows creep where day has died,
In eerie still, where fears reside.
Footsteps echo in the gloom,
From the corners, whispers loom.

Fear's cold fingers clutch the soul,
Every creak, a tale unfolds.
Darkness deepens, breath runs thin,
Haunting nightmares soon begin.

Eyes that pierce through velvet night,
Chasing sanity with fright.
Figures linger 'neath the bed,
Chilling whispers fill the head.

Heartbeats race with every sound,
In the dread, no solace found.
Hold on tight, until the light,
Chase away the endless night.

Solid Ambitions

Dreams are forged in silent shores,
Molding wishes into cores.
Carving paths where none exist,
Strength in will does yet persist.

Brick by brick, the visions rise,
Reaching upward, toward the skies.
Hands that labor, hearts that strive,
Craft ambitions, dreams alive.

With each step, the journey bright,
Set on course with steady might.
Obstacles shall pave the way,
Building futures, day by day.

Solid as the mountains stand,
Firm and steady, grand and planned.
Here we stand, with faith in tow,
Solid dreams begin to grow.

Beyond the Illusion

Past the mirrored, silver screens,
Lies a world beyond our dreams.
Veils of light and shadow play,
Guiding hearts to far away.

Illusions bend and twist the mind,
Tricking senses, rendering blind.
Seek the truth behind the sight,
In the stillness of the night.

Through the fabric, tear the seams,
Hidden layers, unseen themes.
Find the essence, pure and clear,
Past the whispers tinged with fear.

Beyond illusions, find the core,
Realities to once explore.
Tread the path with open eyes,
Truth awaits beyond disguise.

Shadows of Reality

In twilight's gentle embrace,
Where shadows weave and wind,
Reality twists its face,
In realms of the mind.

Beneath the silken night,
Dreams and fears conspire,
Flickers of distant light,
Ignite secretive fire.

Whispers on the breeze,
Echoes of forgotten time,
In this shadowed peace,
Truth and myth entwine.

Masks of the unseen dance,
On the edge of what is known,
Chance and fate's romance,
In shadows they're shown.

Awake in this silent reverie,
Unravel what you see,
For shadows of reality,
Are where the heart is free.

Visions in the Flesh

In the mirror of my soul,
Visions take their form,
Flesh and dreams patrol,
In an endless, shifting storm.

Eyes that pierce the veil,
Glimpse what's deep within,
Stories to unveil,
Where flesh and spirit spin.

Moments carved in skin,
Memories etched in bone,
In the heartbeat's din,
Life's essence overthrown.

Shadows that reflect,
Life's delicate weave,
Spirit and flesh connect,
In the twilight we believe.

In every pulse of being,
A dance of light and dark,
Visions forever seeing,
The undying ember's spark.

Wrens Above Dreams

In earliest dawn's refrain,
Wrens sing soft and sweet,
Above the fields of grain,
Where earth and heavens meet.

Their melodies take flight,
Through hopes and endless streams,
In the soft morning light,
Wrens above dreams.

Beneath the azure sky,
Dreamers set their path,
As wrens on the by and by,
Defy the night's dark wrath.

In each flutter and sway,
Harmony's gentle sweep,
Where wrens and dreams lay,
In realms both vast and deep.

With wings and hearts unbound,
They journey far and wide,
In dreams where wrens are found,
Where peace and love reside.

Solid Whispers

In the hush of night,
Whispers carve their trace,
Solid, clear, and bright,
They find their sacred place.

Echoes of the past,
Speak through lips unseen,
In shadows they will last,
Where thoughts are evergreen.

Each whisper holds a truth,
Unspoken, yet so pure,
In the heart of youth,
Their solid paths endure.

Listen to the silent sound,
Feel it in your core,
Where whispers' truths are found,
On time's ageless shore.

In this quiet exchange,
Lives are intertwined,
Solid whispers arrange,
The dance of heart and mind.

The Weight of Wishes

Beneath the stars, our dreams we swore
In whispered tones where shadows bore
The hopes we dared, the skies we kissed
Now lingered with the weight of wishes

Our silent vows, the winds did keep
In moonlit fields where time's asleep
Remembered now as fleeting blurs
The echoes of our murmured prayers

The night embraced our tender plight
A tapestry of dark and light
With breath held tight, our hearts would sway
To melodies of yesterday

But wishes rest on fragile beams
In secret realms, within our dreams
Unseen, unheard, they softly gleam
In corridors where stardust streams

Yet still we yearn through veil and mist
A futurescape that can't exist
Bound by desires, our souls take flight
Chasing phantoms in the night

Awake in the Imaginary

Through fields of thought where phantoms play
We wander realms of bright array
In spaces carved from dreams anew
Where every whisper feels like you

With eyes half-closed, the mind unfolds
A theater where no tale grows old
Each story spins in endless dance
In corridors of happenstance

Awake, we drift through painted streams
Beside the shores of unseen dreams
In silent reverie, hearts beat
To rhythms soft but bittersweet

There, time stands still, a grace so pure
In shadows deep where gleam obscured
Imaginary worlds unfurl
Their mysteries a sacred pearl

As dawn arrives, reality
Intrudes on fragile reverie
Yet echoes linger, softly stay
Awake in dreams, we find our way

Essence in Illusion

In twilight hours where silence sings
The essence of illusions springs
A dance of light, a whispered chord
In shadows where our truths are stored

With fragile grace, illusions wane
They weave through moments, yet remain
A fleeting glimpse, a tender sight
Dissolving in the velvet night

In every shade of dusk's embrace
The edges blur, and time we trace
Fleeting as a phantom's sigh
We pass through realms of reasons why

Beneath the moon's soft guiding glow
Illusions deep, we come to know
A symphony of dreams profound
Where hidden truths and myths abound

The essence held in hands unseen
A delicate, elusive sheen
Though wisps and whispers, they distort
Our hearts still seek their true rapport

Living in Layers

We live in layers, masks adorned
With faces new for each new morn
Beneath the surface, dreams repose
In silent places no one knows

Each day a new façade we wear
A shift of tones, of masks we bear
From dawn to dusk in swirling hues
We dance, we change, we sometimes lose

Within, our true selves softly call
In whispers that, aloud, seem small
Yet through the layers, deep we dive
To find the spark that keeps us alive

A mosaic of our crafted scenes
Of half-truths, hopes, and hidden means
Yet in each layer, fragments lie
Of who we are, of reasons why

A journey through these veils, we take
In quest of self, no longer fake
Living in layers helps us see
The multifaceted beauty of 'me'

Curtains of Reality

Veils of illusion fall, unseen,
As truth emerges, bold and clean.
Shadows dance in flickered light,
Revealing depths of endless night.

Through silken threads we weave our dreams,
In silent whispers, life redeems.
A tapestry of hopes unfurled,
Curtains rise; behold the world.

Secrets hide in folds of time,
Ancient tales in cryptic rhyme.
Reality obscure and true,
Curtains part to clearer view.

Mysteries known and yet concealed,
In twilight's glow, all is revealed.
Curtains sway with gentle grace,
Unveiling life's timeless face.

With each breath, new vistas birth,
Curtains shift 'tween heaven, earth.
Reality, a fleeting gaze,
In cosmic dance, our minds amaze.

Actuality Behind the Veil

A mystic shroud, the world confounds,
Hiding secrets in its bounds.
Behind the veil, the essence lies,
Truth reflected in our eyes.

Beyond the mist of fleeting dreams,
Reality more vivid seems.
In shadows cast by morning sun,
Begins a journey, once begun.

Through veils, a whisper calls our name,
A spark ignites the inner flame.
Actuality's tender touch,
A presence felt within us much.

Unraveling the woven thread,
We find the truths we often dread.
Behind the surface, raw and plain,
Actuality breaks its chain.

Embrace the world in purest form,
Through life's storm, a calm reborn.
The veil is thin, the heart can see,
Actuality, wild and free.

Beating Heart of Reverie

In realms where dreams and visions play,
A beating heart does find its way.
Reveries bloom in silent night,
A dance of shadows, soft and light.

In whispered thoughts, desires grow,
Through timeless fields where breezes blow.
A heart that beats in endless song,
A reverie, both wild and strong.

In twilight's hush, a dream takes flight,
Through star-lit paths of pure delight.
The heart that guides, as if by grace,
Through reverie's gentle embrace.

With every pulse, a world anew,
Of colors bright and feelings true.
A harmony in silent plea,
The beating heart of reverie.

Awake, the soul in dreams does soar,
A beating heart forever more.
In realms unseen, where hopes reside,
In reverie, we thus abide.

Material Echoes

In the quiet, a whisper starts,
Echoes born from ancient hearts.
Material forms from shadows cast,
A bridge from present to the past.

Each touch, a memory's gentle claim,
To ages past, we lend our name.
Through echoes, voices softly weave,
The stories time would not bereave.

In stones and wood, in earth below,
Material echoes softly flow.
A trace of lives once lived and gone,
Within the present softly drawn.

With care, we tread on whispered dreams,
In tangible, elusive streams.
Material echoes, loud and clear,
Remind us of what we hold dear.

In every breath, a past revived,
Material echoes, thus contrived.
A legacy in whispers told,
Through echoes, histories unfold.

Concrete Fantasies

Cities rise from dreams of old
Steel and glass, both hot and cold
Echoes whisper, sidewalks scream
In this modern, fervent dream

Bricks and mortar, souls entwined
Lives unfolded, paths aligned
Beneath the neon, shadows play
Turning night into the day

Windows glitter, stories told
In their frame, the world's unfold
Skyscrapers reach for skies so blue
Concrete whispers, ever true

Pavement hums with constant life
Joy, and sorrow, peace, and strife
Beneath the surface, hearts pulsate
In this pulse, we navigate

From the heights, the city glows
And as above, so below
Concrete fantasies, alive
Where the human spirits thrive

Living the Dream Awake

Morning kisses skies so bright
Dreams dissolve in morning light
Eyes wide open, hearts do soar
Living life, we dream for more

Sunrise casts a golden hue
Promises of all things new
In each heartbeat, dreams reside
In each step, we hearts confide

Planted seeds in fertile ground
In our souls, the roots are found
Growing tall and reaching high
On these dreams, we learn to fly

Awake and dreaming, we pursue
All the colors in the blue
Every star, a goal in sight
In the vastness, we alight

Living the dream, wide awake
Every moment, breath we take
A tapestry of hope we weave
In this life, our dreams conceive

Fragments of the Now

Moments crash like waves to shore
Each a piece, but never more
In their passing, time is curved
In their essence, life is served

Shattered seconds form a whole
Bits of time, they shape the soul
In the now, we find our place
In each moment's warm embrace

Ephemeral, the fleeting trace
Of the smiles upon a face
In these fragments, time suspends
Moments infinite, transcends

Catching glimpses of the now
In the present, we avow
Lives are lived in these brief sparks
Guiding through the darkened parks

Time a river, always flows
In each fragment, life bestows
In the present, we are blessed
In the now, our hearts find rest

Tangible Visions

Dreams with substance, solid made
In the daylight, shadows fade
Tangible, each vision born
In the light of early morn

Touch the vision, feel its core
Inspiration, wanting more
Shapes and colors, forms aligned
In this realm, our dreams unwind

From the mind to matter shift
In each thought, there's a gift
Crafted hopes and sculpted dreams
Manifest in sunlight streams

Built from whispers, forged anew
In each act, the visions brew
Tangible and firmly set
In our grasp, our dreams beget

From the abstract, concrete grows
In these visions, life bestows
Each creation, hand in hand
Tangible, our dreams expand

Beneath the Ethereal

A silken glow, the stars do weave,
Through midnight's veil, they brightly cleave.
In whispers soft, the cosmos sigh,
As dreamers gaze and wonders pry.

The moonlight drapes on silver tides,
Unfolding tales that time confides.
Above the clouds, where angels croon,
An ethered dance, a mystic tune.

With every breath, the night expands,
Awakening lands, unseen by hands.
Beneath the ethereal, boundless dreams,
Where silence hums and starlight gleams.

The nebulous words, the night confers,
In cosmic tongues, that wind prefers.
In shadows deep, where secrets keep,
The heart of night begins to leap.

Upon this stage, the universe,
In silent verse, our thoughts immerse.
Within its fold, the spirit yields,
To mysteries that midnight shields.

Visions Concretized

In cityscapes of steel and glass,
Where shadows dance as seconds pass.
Conceiving dreams in bricks and stone,
Where hopes and fears are not alone.

Through beating hearts of metronomes,
The city's pulse, a thousand tomes.
Visions rise in structured frames,
A dance of lights, a realm of names.

Concrete jungles, towering high,
Whispers caught between the sky.
Within its grid, ambitions writhe,
Each breath a testament to strive.

The morning sun on window panes,
Illuminates the hidden chains.
In paths we carve and sawdust trails,
Our visions anchor, never fail.

Yet in the night, when calm descends,
These constructs bend where silence bends.
Concrete visions crystallize,
As dreams unfurl to touch the skies.

Beyond the Mirage

In desert lands, where shadows play,
The fleeting edge of night and day.
Mirrors dance on golden sands,
As whispers drift from distant lands.

The heat sings songs, the air does waver,
In mirage forms, our senses savor.
A distant lake, an oasis near,
Beckons calls, both far and clear.

Yet closer still, the vision fades,
Within the weave, where light cascades.
Reality cloaked in desert's haze,
A transient ghost in sunlit ways.

Beyond the mirage, the truth is born,
From shifting sands and skies forlorn.
Seek within the heart of dreams,
The thread of life in sunlit seems.

With every step and every breath,
Unveil the paths where shadows rest.
Beyond the mirage, a world revealed,
In truth and light, our fate is sealed.

Reality Underneath Dreams

In twilight's glow, where dreams take flight,
Beyond the veils of silent night.
Through whispered fields and shadowed streams,
Lie truths untold, beneath our dreams.

Within the slumber's gentle clasp,
We touch the stars, the heavens grasp.
Yet underneath, a layer's deep,
Where waking dawns and visions seep.

From ethered lands of mind's creation,
Flows the river of sensation.
Reality anchors where dreams unfurl,
Beneath the currents, life's a whirl.

In every pulse, the heart conceives,
A world where waking soul believes.
Yet dreams reshape the firmest ground,
In shifting hues, the truth is found.

Awake to find in morning's light,
The dreamt illusions of the night.
Reality beneath these schemes,
A whispered song, in waking dreams.

Moments Beyond Mirage

Fleeting shadows dance on golden sands,
Whispers of dreams in distant lands.
Ephemeral glows, the sun's embrace,
Moments etched in twilight's grace.

Ripples on time's eternal stream,
Echoes linger of a wandering dream.
In mirage and mist, truth finds its trace,
Woven threads of past's sweet lace.

Glistening dew on petals' edge,
Promises whispered, an unbroken pledge.
Mirages fade, but memories stay,
Guiding light on a moonlit bay.

In the silence, the heart's true plea,
Beyond illusions, the soul runs free.
Time weaves its tapestry grand,
Moments caught in the shifting sand.

Endless horizons, skies unfurled,
In mirage, discover the world's true pearl.
In every shift and every tide,
Moments beyond, where dreams reside.

Actual Breath

In the quiet hush of dawn's fresh air,
Life awakens, with nary a care.
Breaths untangled from night's dark weave,
Moments cherished beyond belief.

Each inhale brings the world anew,
Exhale whispers dreams come true.
In this rhythm, hearts find their beat,
Simple joys, a treasure to keep.

Within each breath, a promise lies,
Hope beneath expansive skies.
Every sigh, a silent prayer,
Breathing in love's tender care.

As the world turns, a constant hum,
Breath by breath, we overcome.
In and out, a dance so vast,
Moments savored, futures cast.

Inhale the essence, exhale the strife,
In breath's embrace, discover life.
Actual breaths become our creed,
Nurturing hearts, planting seeds.

Concrete Cascade

In urban sprawl, where shadows weave,
Silent rivers in the concrete seethe.
Towers rise, a man-made blade,
In steel and glass, dreams cascade.

City murmurs, an endless hum,
Lives entwine in a mechanical drum.
Beneath the surface, stories flow,
Echoes of time, seeds that grow.

In alleyways, where secrets lie,
A cascade of hopes reach the sky.
Building bridges, minds convene,
Concrete pulses, unseen, serene.

Every stone, a piece of lore,
Every path, an open door.
In the cascade, futures blend,
Concrete dreams with no end.

Structures loom, yet hearts remain,
In concrete vastness, find the humane.
In every cascade, a leap of faith,
Endless echoes, life in wraith.

Substance in the Shade

In shadows deep, where light retreats,
Substance whispers, life's concealed beats.
Hidden treasures, truths unfold,
In shade's embrace, stories told.

Beneath the canopy of silence dense,
Life's essence weaves, intense, immense.
From hushed tones to whispers serene,
Substance blooms, a hidden sheen.

In the quiet, strength emerges neat,
Roots from shadows, deeply seat.
Shade may cloak, but does not fade,
Substance thrives, ever conveyed.

A quiet nook, where souls align,
Shade relieves, hearts combine.
In the depths, perception takes hold,
Rich substance, not timid or cold.

Explore the shade, where depth resides,
Find the keeps, the hearts that hide.
Substance nurtured, steadfast, unmade,
True essence, in the shade.

Breathing Illusions

In hushed twilight, shadows dance,
A masquerade of silk and air.
Breathing lies in every glance,
Whispers echo everywhere.

Mirrors hold the fragile veil,
Of truths that linger just beyond.
Reality seems to pale,
In illusions we're so fond.

Skies of shifting, mottled hue,
Crafting figments soft and bright.
What is false and what is true?
Both entwined with all our might.

Dreams are painted, fleeting art,
On the canvas of the night.
Silent breaths that tease the heart,
Lost in the unearthly light.

In illusions we find hope,
A gentle breath to soothe the mind.
On this tightrope, do we cope,
With the truths we're yet to find?

Grit in the Gossamer

Midst the silken webs we weave,
Lies a thread so coarse and wild.
Hidden truths we can't conceive,
Yet to them, we are beguiled.

Gossamer around the heart,
In its fragility, there's strength.
From the whole, each rugged part,
Dares to go to great lengths.

Dust of dreams and drops of dew,
On the delicate threads we spin.
Each grain of truth breaks through,
Grit and grace, both therein.

Veils of light and shadows clash,
Tales of the raw and refined.
In each glow, a sudden flash,
Of consciousness redefined.

Through the delicate we tread,
Seeking what is frail and firm.
In the web, the grit we spread,
Life's entangled, endless term.

Echoes of Material

Whispers linger in the stone,
Tales of time and vast expanse.
Every creak and every moan,
Echoes of a hidden dance.

In the fabric, in the clay,
Stories wait to be unfurled.
Simple things have much to say,
In a fleeting, changing world.

Metal sings when struck by light,
A resonance that's tightly bound.
Echoes ringing through the night,
In each shape a subtle sound.

Wooden grains and crystal tears,
Hold the secrets we pursue.
Through the fabric of the years,
Materials speak what's true.

In each echo, a refrain,
Of the life within the form.
Timeless lessons to sustain,
Bearing calm within the storm.

Substance in Dreams

Woven in the fabric thin,
Are the dreams we dare to chase.
In their midst, where do we begin?
Each desire softly traced.

Flickers in the night unfold,
Images both grand and slight.
In the darkness, visions bold,
Shaping form from hidden light.

Tangible yet out of reach,
Dreams are made of things unseen.
They are pathways they each teach,
Realities laced between.

In the waking world we tread,
Holding dreams within our palms.
Substance in each word we've said,
As we seek the deeper calms.

In the dreams we find the thread,
That connects to all that's real.
In their substance, truths are bred,
Guiding us in ways we feel.

Heartbeats in the Haze

In the twilight's dim embrace,
Shadows dance, elusive, frail.
Whispers echo, hearts retrace,
Every beat, a whispered tale.

Clouds obscure the distant moon,
Mystic pulses in the night.
Lovers' songs in tender tune,
Guiding souls to morning's light.

Veils of dreams begin to lift,
Gentle sighs, the night's soft call.
In the haze, emotions drift,
Catching hearts before they fall.

Stars that blink in silent skies,
Hold the secrets we confide.
Through the mist, where truth resides,
Heartbeats in the haze collide.

Luminous Truths

Glints of gold in dawn's first light,
Reveal the truths we seek to hide.
Shimmering truths in plainest sight,
Reflections of our deepest tide.

Through the fog of doubt and fear,
Clarity, like sunbeams, break.
Illuminating paths we steer,
With every honest step we take.

Underneath the shadowed veil,
Lies a world of radiant grace.
Hidden stories, dreams unveiled,
In every line upon our face.

Bright the truths that bring us peace,
Lighting up the darkest night.
In the stillness, whispers cease,
Luminous in honest light.

Emergence from Fantasy

From the dreams where we reside,
Reality begins to bloom.
Bridges built where hearts collide,
Specters fade from shadowed gloom.

Waking from a world of mist,
To the brilliance of the day.
Truth and fantasy coexist,
Yet it's time to find our way.

In the quiet of the dawn,
We feel the gentle rise of hope.
Fantasy now fades, withdrawn,
Leaving us with room to cope.

Emergence from the world of night,
Breathes new life into our souls.
Guided by the morning light,
Fantasy to truth consoles.

Grounded Imagination

Wings that span the endless sky,
Yet our roots are strong, profound.
Grounded dreams that soar and fly,
Where both earth and stars are found.

Imagination takes its flight,
From the soil of what is real.
Weaving daydreams in the night,
Grounded in the things we feel.

Listeners of the wild air,
Hear the whispers of the ground.
In the stillness, finding there,
Dreams and truths in harmony bound.

Earth and sky, they intertwine,
Balance in a dance divine.
Grounded heart and wandering mind,
In imagination's rhymed design.

Mirror of Certainty

In a glassy pool I see,
My reflection stares at me,
Truth and doubt in symmetry,
Bound by fate eternally.

Ripples shift the mirrored face,
Timeless whispers leave a trace,
Questions asked in silent grace,
Answers float in empty space.

Every glance a tale unfolds,
Every secret darkness holds,
Future paths the water molds,
Mystery of life unfolds.

Certainty in shadows cast,
Echoes of the future's past,
Moments fleeting, never last,
In the mirror's truth amass.

Reality and dreams entwine,
In the depths, reflections shine,
Every edge a thin, fine line,
Certainty and fate combine.

Flesh and Dreams

In the realm of midnight's peace,
Flesh meets dreams, a sweet release,
Whispers through the world's crease,
In the night, all worries cease.

Visions dance with muted grace,
Fleeting shadows, a tender trace,
Worlds beyond in soft embrace,
In slumber's hold, we find our place.

Every heartbeat tells a tale,
In our sleep, we set our sail,
Through the stars, beyond the pale,
Dreams and flesh in parallel.

Eyes closed tight, the soul takes flight,
Skies of wonder, realms of light,
In this world of pure delight,
Bound by day, free by night.

Morning comes, the dreamscape fades,
Reality in light cascades,
Yet the dreams, like softly played,
In our hearts, forever stays.

Grounded Visions

Feet on earth, eyes on the sky,
Dreams take wings, ambitions fly,
Grounded souls that seek to try,
Reaching high, we question why.

Mountains tall and valleys deep,
Promises the night will keep,
In our quest, no time for sleep,
Visions held, memories steep.

Every step a journey starts,
Hope and love in human hearts,
Crafting dreams like ancient arts,
Building bridges, mending parts.

Challenges along our way,
Teach us more than words can say,
Through the night and into day,
Grounded visions lead our way.

Bound by earth yet touching stars,
Journey takes us near and far,
Truth and dreams in who we are,
Guided by a distant star.

Solid Silhouettes

Against the orange evening glow,
Silhouettes in silence show,
Stories carved in shadow's flow,
Figures stand, steadfastly grow.

Every shape a life's refrain,
Movements captured, moments gain,
Traces left by joy and pain,
Solid forms in twilight's reign.

Silent echoes, time stands still,
Shapes of dreams and iron will,
In the calm, our souls refill,
Underneath the moonlit hill.

Bound by earth yet free in mind,
Tales of old and new combined,
Through the dark, the stars aligned,
Silhouettes in shadows find.

Life in darkness softly set,
Bound by love and faint regret,
In the twilight, we are met,
Figures formed, solid silhouettes.

Reality in Color

In shades of blue, we find the sky,
Where whispers of the wind pass by,
Emerald grass beneath our feet,
A world in color, bold and sweet.

The crimson hues of dawn's first light,
Awaken dreams yet out of sight,
Through golden fields, we chase the day,
In vibrant hues, we find our way.

Soft lavender in twilight's glow,
Brings serene peace, as night winds blow,
In every hue, a tale unfolds,
Reality in colors bold.

Turquoise oceans vast and deep,
Hold secrets in their waters' keep,
With each hue, our spirits soar,
In colors, there's always more.

Amber leaves in autumn's reign,
A fleeting beauty, joy with pain,
In their descent, to earth they fall,
Reality in colors calls.

Manifested Hopes

In dreams, we plant our seeds of gold,
Hopes that with the dawn unfold,
In fields of mind, they take their root,
From silent thoughts, they start to shoot.

With every sunrise, faith renewed,
In morning's light, our dreams are cued,
The world conspires to help them grow,
Manifested hopes start to show.

Through trials fierce, and storms unkind,
In perseverance, strength we find,
Emerging through the darkest nights,
Are hopes aglow with life's own lights.

In whispers of the evening breeze,
Promises hang upon the trees,
Every leaf a granted prayer,
Manifested hopes float in air.

The stars above in silent cheer,
Reflect the hopes we've held so dear,
With open hearts, we greet the dawn,
Manifested hopes, new lives drawn.

Echoes of Today

Beneath the sun's relentless glare,
In shadowed corners, joy and care,
The moments of a life, refined,
Echoes of today, in time.

Each heartbeat like a drum's soft beat,
Marking the rhythm, strong yet sweet,
In every breath, a tale we weave,
Echoes of today, we leave.

Voices merge in a crowded street,
Untold stories, paths that meet,
In every face, a glimpse, a play,
Echoes of today, on display.

In laughter's tone or sorrow's sigh,
In dreams that reach beyond the sky,
The present's essence, bold and clear,
Echoes of today, we hear.

In quiet moments just before,
The dusk arrives, and day is o'er,
Reflections of our hearts, convey,
The echoes of our precious today.

Dreams Carved in Stone

On ancient walls, through hands of time,
Dreams etched in stone in rhythm and rhyme,
With every chisel, hope takes form,
A legacy amidst the storm.

In monuments both grand and small,
Whispers of dreams that dare to call,
As mountains rise, so do our schemes,
Forever carved in timeless dreams.

Through granite strong and marble pure,
Ambitions bold and hearts that cure,
The stones remember dreams of old,
Stories of courage, brave and bold.

With every mark, a promise made,
In granite lines that never fade,
From dreams once whispered, now on high,
Carved in stone, they touch the sky.

In twilight's glow, when day is done,
And moonlight bathes the world as one,
We read the dreams that stones have borne,
A testament to lives reborn.

Flesh Over Phantoms

Between the mists of dream and dawn,
A figure stands both clear and wan.
Whispered words of skin and bone,
Walks the earth, towards the unknown.

Echoes of a life, unreal,
Drifting past the touch and feel.
Reach out, grasp the solid air,
Flesh over phantoms, dare to care.

Eyes that see beyond the veil,
Heartbeats carve the fragile trail.
Reality and ghostly ties,
In a dance that never dies.

Hands that brush against the past,
Hold onto the moments cast.
Treading paths both new and old,
In the warmth, a tale is told.

Timeless spirits whisper low,
Painted hues of life's tableau.
Tangible the breath and sigh,
Flesh over phantoms, reaching high.

Touch of the Mirage

Desert winds that weave and sing,
Ephemeral, the mirage brings.
Visions shimmer in the heat,
Illusions tempt at weary feet.

Crystal pools that reflect the sky,
Disappear as you draw nigh.
Soft as dreams and hard as stone,
A fleeting world you walk alone.

Palms that fade beneath the sun,
Oasis gleams, yet it is none.
Reach out, trace the phantom's edge,
Beyond the lie, a silent pledge.

Spectral hands that lead the day,
Ephemeral and slow to stay.
Golden sands that whisper low,
In mirage's gentle flow.

Touch it once, it slips away,
In your heart, the dreams will stay.
Mirage or true, it matters not,
In the touch, all's forgot.

Glimmer of the Actual

In a world of shades and dust,
Find the treasures, find the trust.
Golden hints of what is real,
Glimmering through the truths we feel.

Light that dances, pure and bright,
Through the darkest, quiet night.
Emerald leaves and sapphire skies,
True as love that never lies.

Moments fleeting, yet they burn,
In the hearts that always yearn.
Glimmers caught in every eye,
Sparks of truth that never die.

Fragments of reality,
Pieced together, set you free.
Hold them close and hold them dear,
Glimmer of the actual, here.

Cherish what the real reveals,
In its glimmers, life appeals.
Stronger than the shadows cast,
Reality's glimmer, hold it fast.

Dew on Real Leaves

Morning light that softly falls,
On dewdrops' crystalline recalls.
Every leaf, a shimmering grace,
Reflects the dawn upon its face.

Whispers of the night before,
In droplets hang, forevermore.
True as day and true as time,
Each one holds a silent rhyme.

Touched by rays of golden morn,
Nature's jewels are gently worn.
Glistening on the verdant green,
Echoes of a world unseen.

Softly tread where dew is laid,
Nature's beauty, unafraid.
Real as breath and real as life,
In each drop, there is no strife.

Morning's kiss, a promise keeps,
In the dew, the realness seeps.
Truth in nature, truth in sight,
Dew on real leaves, pure delight.

Dreamscapes with Roots

In twilight's tender embrace, I stand
Between the worlds of earth and sky
Roots dig deep in the fertile land
As dreams like stars above me lie

I close my eyes and feel the pull
Of whispered truths in evening's glow
Through soil and clouds, a symphony full
A song that only dreamers know

With every breath, the roots grow tight
Binding me to earth's gentle care
Yet in the vast, expanse of night
Boundless dreams drift everywhere

Anchored by love and courage bold
I walk the path of moonlit beams
In lands both new and ancient, told
I find the roots of all my dreams

Eternal threads weave night's embrace
In quiet realms where dreams take root
A dance of stars, of silken lace
Lays bare the soul's most precious fruit

Grounded Mesmerization

Underneath the city's whispered hum
Life unfurls in secret, hidden bands
A world beneath where roots become
the keepers of our time-worn lands

Each step on cobblestone and clay
Resounds through veins of buried lore
In every crack, the earth's display
A mesmerizing hidden core

Velvet shadows weave their charm
Like fingers through the downy earth
Keeping us safe from thought of harm
In lullabies of nature's birth

We walk on dreams entwined with soil
As roots hold tight in quiet grace
The ground, its magic will not spoil
In every crevice, safe embrace

Silent guardians, ancient, wise
Roots unseen, but strong, unfazed
Hold us in their gentle ties
With earth's mesmerization swayed

Touching Skylines

Above the rooftops, 'neath the sun-kissed hue
Where sky meets earth in bold designs
My spirit soars on wings anew
Through endless, touching skylines

With every rise and fall of light
The horizon stretches, unconfined
Inviting dreams to take their flight
And paint the heavens in kind

From morning's veil to dusk's retreat
Colors bleed in passionate swirls
As visions rise on air so sweet
Embracing all the world unfurls

Each skyline holds a secret thread
That binds the earth to dreams above
Where hopes and fears in twilight spread
In hues of wonder, tales of love

I touch the sky, my spirit free
In endless realms where visions twine
From dawn to dusk, in unity
I'm home within these touching skylines

Ephemeral Roots

Beneath the surface, life's fine threads
they weave a tale of fleeting grace
Ephemeral roots in silken beds
hold time's embrace, a fragile lace

Like whispers on the autumn breeze
These roots entwine, both light and true
In moments lost among the trees
They find the soils they once knew

Transient in their paths below
They pulse with life, then drift away
A dance of roots that softly flow
Through earth's embrace, they cannot stay

Each root a fleeting song of earth
A melody of growth and then
Returns to dust, of fated birth
Joining the cycles once again

In every root's ephemeral flight
A testament to life's refrain
A moment grasped in fading light
Then softly gone, yet not in vain

Embodying the Abstract

In whispers of the silent air,
Where unseen thoughts take flight,
Ideas shape, beyond compare,
A canvas born of light.

A shadow cast without a source,
A bridge with no clear end,
Mysteries chart their hidden course,
Concepts intertwine, transcend.

In every breath, a spectrum blooms,
Colors of the mind's deep hold,
Eclipsing time in myriad rooms,
New stories to be told.

Unseen patterns weave their thread,
Through vast expanses, unexplored,
Mindscapes rise where dreams are bred,
The abstract is restored.

Eyes closed, yet vision clear,
In realms where logic bends,
Embrace the thought, dispel the fear,
Where the surreal descends.

Substance in Ephemera

A fleeting touch, a whispered name,
Such moments carve the heart,
In transient glows, arise the flame,
Whose warmth will ne'er depart.

Ephemeral joys, like morning dew,
That glisten with the dawn,
In fragile webs, our spirits strew,
Where timeless threads are drawn.

A summer breeze, a winter sigh,
Both linger, then they fade,
Yet in their wake, emotions lie,
With memories gently laid.

The beauty in the brief encounter,
Leaves echoes, bittersweet,
In each embrace, we are the counter,
To time's relentless beat.

So cherish now the fleeting glance,
The moment, light and pure,
In shadows cast by happenstance,
Eternity is sure.

Timeless Flesh

Beneath the skin where secrets hide,
Within each cell, time's tale,
A legacy of life's great stride,
In flesh we cannot fail.

From ancient lands, our forebears call,
Through beating hearts, they sing,
Their essence flows, and through us all,
Eternity takes wing.

Each wrinkle worn, a silent scream,
Of battles long since won,
Through vibrant lives, the ageless dream,
We pass from sire to son.

In every scar, a story told,
Of life, in all its strife,
In flesh, the young and aged hold,
The essence of their life.

So in the mirror, see not the wear,
But histories tightly spun,
In timeless flesh, we know we're there,
When all is said and done.

Gossamer Made Solid

As dreams descend on midnight's veil,
And visions gently weave,
Each fragile thread begins the tale,
Of more than we believe.

In silken strands that shimmer bright,
The ghostly hopes reside,
Like moonbeams dancing through the night,
To where illusions bide.

A web of mist, yet strong as steel,
In gossamer, truth bold,
What once seemed fake begins to feel,
A story to be told.

Transmute the haze to solid form,
Through will, through endless might,
Reality in dreams is born,
When shadows come to light.

From fleeting thought to sturdy frame,
The gossamer made strong,
In fragile webs, we stake our claim,
And know where we belong.

Chasing Tangibility

In dreams ethereal, we often find
A longing for what's vividly entwined
With senses sharp, our visions dance
Chasing tangibility with each chance

Through mists of hope, our souls do wade
Seeking forms from thoughts carefully laid
The abstract yearns for concrete shape
To feel, to hold, an endless gape

Minds paint landscapes so sublime
Only to fade in fleeting time
Yet, in the heart, remains the quest
Chasing tangibility without rest

Each whisper of reality, so near
Bears the weight of silent fear
Will dreams dissolve in morning light
Or form at dawn, pure and bright?

Hands reach out to grasp the air
Through faith, through doubt, the truth lay bare
Chasing tangibility, we persist
For what we seek must coexist

From Thought to Touch

In the haven of a silent mind
Ideas blossom, unconstrained, unlined
They yearn to breach the veil of thought
From shadow's edge, to light be brought

Threads of imagination weave
Tapestries we can perceive
From thought to touch, the journey grand
To cradle dreams within our hand

Every whisper of the inner soul
Seeks a form, a tangible goal
Through twists of fate, through turns of time
Thoughts transform in the heart's prime

With courage as the guiding light
We sculpt the day from silent night
From thought to touch, we dare to leap
To hold the dreams we've sown so deep

In this dance of hope and fear
The abstract world becomes so clear
From thought to touch, a final step
Amid the bounds where souls are kept

Actualized Aspirations

In the forge of ambitions bright
We mold our dreams with fierce delight
Actualized aspirations climb
Beyond the bounds of space and time

Eyes set upon the distant shore
Waves of hope that ever-more
Will rise to meet the sky's embrace
To find in life a sacred place

The echo of our silent plea
To shape the world as it should be
Each cherished wish takes form and flight
Through shadows deep, into the light

With hands that craft and minds that dream
We navigate the endless stream
Actualized aspirations become our guide
In them, our deepest truths reside

Celestial paths we bravely chart
With every beat of faithful heart
Actualized aspirations soar
To realms of life where spirits roar

Dimensional Musings

In realms unseen by mortal eyes
Where dreams take flight, where hope applies
Dimensional musings, thoughts so free
Traverse the bounds of what's to be

The present, past, and future blend
Timelines that curve and never end
Infinite paths the mind can trace
Seeking truths in boundless space

With each musing, worlds are born
In twilight's light and breaking morn
Dimensions shift, new forms arise
Shaped by belief, truth, and lies

The universe reflects our quest
In every thought, we manifest
Dimensional musings whisper clear
In realms where futures reappear

Lost in space of inner glow
Where endless possibilities grow
Dimensional musings softly gleam
To weave the fabric of our dream

Reflections of Existence

In the quiet of the mind, thoughts take flight,
Seeking the depth of life's twilight,
Mirrors of time, they gently show,
Faces we've met, places we'd go.

In shadows cast by eternity's glow,
Moments whisper, ebb, and flow,
Reflections dance on existence's stream,
Where heart and soul in silence dream.

Every memory a ripple's grace,
Waves of history, time's embrace,
In the stillness, truth unfurls,
The essence of our transient worlds.

The past and future softly blend,
In the present, we find our end,
Journey endless, yet so brief,
Within our thoughts lie belief.

Mirror images, lives turned pages,
Stories told through endless ages,
Reflections, mirrors of our being,
In their depth, life worth seeing.

Vivid Yet Real

Colors dance on twilight's sky,
Dreams awaken, dare to fly,
Vivid hues, our hearts precise,
In every shade, life does arise.

The world a canvas, bolder brush,
Every moment an artist's hush,
Vivid scenes in silent reel,
Life's a dream but yet, it's real.

In the stillness, hues collide,
Vivid dreams are our guide,
Reality and fantasy blend,
Where waking lives and dreams transcend.

Eyes wide open, visions clear,
Every day, a frontier near,
Vivid imaginings, thoughts congealed,
In each heartbeat, life's revealed.

Truth in art, both live and frame,
Vivid tales in passion's flame,
Yet in dreams, the real concealed,
Life's pure essence once revealed.

Solid Reveries

Building castles in the air,
Dreams of light, beyond compare,
Solid forms from thoughts arise,
In waking worlds, they crystallize.

Clouds of wonder, firmament bound,
Where whispered hopes and dreams are found,
Solid reveries, they take their stand,
Crafting life with unseen hands.

Night and day, the lines do blur,
Solid dreams in hearts confer,
Foundations built on fleeting sighs,
Reveries where solid truths lie.

Reality in every thought,
Solid visions gently wrought,
Dreams and life's entwining streams,
Waking moments, solid dreams.

Within our minds, realms so vast,
Solid reveries hold fast,
Every stone a whispered plea,
Dreams become reality.

Truths Beyond Clouds

Storms may gather, clouds may rise,
Truth lies hidden in the skies,
Beyond the shadows, light reveals,
All the strength our heart conceals.

Whispers through the tempest's call,
Truths beyond the stormy squall,
Every cloud a passing veil,
Through it all, our truths prevail.

Hidden suns will shine anew,
Beyond the gray, the skies so blue,
In the storm's eye, peace found there,
Truths beyond, beyond compare.

The heavens speak in silent tones,
Truths in whispers, undertones,
Beyond the clouds, a world divine,
Hidden paths for hearts to find.

In between the drops of rain,
Truths of life in soft refrain,
Every storm will cease, allow,
To find the light beyond the clouds.

Textures of the Real

The fabric of days, so rich and so vast,
Unfolds in layers, a narrative cast.
Beneath the surface, truths reveal,
In textures felt, the pulse of the real.

Moments weave threads in a tapestry great,
Colors of joy, sorrow, love, and fate.
The unseen hands that craft with zeal,
A masterpiece known as the real.

In every sigh, in every stare,
Lie stories hidden, unaware.
In the quiet, do we feel,
The intricate dance of the real.

A touch, a glance, a whispered phrase,
Illuminate life's obscure maze.
Life's textures, in rush or still,
Mold the essence, firm and real.

Canvas of life, both rough and smooth,
Each wrinkle and crease, with meaning soothes.
Embrace the chaos, the wounds that heal,
And find in the threads, textures real.

Actualized Whispers

Voices soft as the twilight air,
In quiet quite they do declare.
Dreams once hidden, shyly rise,
From whispering winds, hopes actualize.

In the stillness, secrets speak,
Of future's path, both bright and bleak.
From the shadows that disguise,
The heart's true song, whispers actualize.

Silent echoes from the deep,
Promises they've sworn to keep.
Whispered dreams where truth lies,
In the dawn, they actualize.

Through the night, soft murmurs sail,
Carrying wishes, frail and pale.
In the morn, beneath clear skies,
Whispered bonds, they actualize.

Words unspoken find their way,
Into the light of breaking day.
From the stillness, to the skies,
All that's whispered, actualized.

Living the Unseen

In shadows cast, where light is rare,
Exist the forms, beyond compare.
Unspoken truths, in the in-between,
We find our souls, living the unseen.

In quiet nooks and silent rooms,
Beneath the stars, the unseen blooms.
Life whispers softly, moments glean,
From hidden realms, living the unseen.

In the spaces, time forgot,
Lies the essence of each thought.
In the margins, dreams convene,
Whispered breaths, living the unseen.

Through veils of mist, through curtains drawn,
There's a world before the dawn.
In this realm, pure and serene,
We discover life, living the unseen.

Beneath the world's loud, glaring light,
Lie shadows deep, profound as night.
Journey inward, past routine,
To the heart of life's unseen.

The Concrete Ethereal

Foundations built on dreams so high,
In the realm where heavens lie.
Tangible worlds, firmly surreal,
Craft the essence, concrete ethereal.

Bridges span the voids of thought,
Connect the realms that time forgot.
In every stone, in every seal,
Resides the spirit, concrete ethereal.

Through the structures rise and fall,
Echoes of the hopeful call.
In their strength, do we feel,
The sacred bond, concrete ethereal.

Urban jungles whisper lore,
Of ancient hearts forevermore.
In the metal, glass, and steel,
Lives the mystic, concrete ethereal.

Realities that blend and shift,
In every crafted, earthly gift.
Mortal dreams in forms reveal,
The silent song, concrete ethereal.

Sewn with Substance

Threads of gold on fabric's grace,
Weaving tales in silent space,
Every stitch a crafted lore,
Binding dreams forevermore.

Fingers dance with needle's glide,
Patterns form, thoughts coincide,
Seams that whisper, folds embrace,
Crafted moments held in lace.

Time stitched into every fold,
Stories ancient yet untold,
Woven bonds of love and care,
Textures rich, beyond compare.

Draped in cloth, the past survives,
In each hem, a spirit thrives,
From loom to heart, essence flows,
In the fabric, life bestows.

Sewn with substance, depth refined,
In each thread, connection finds,
Tangled art in layers wide,
In this quilt, memories reside.

Anchored Whimsy

A ship of dreams on ocean's tide,
With sails of stardust, vast and wide,
Anchored deep in realms of thought,
A vessel where the wild is caught.

Breezes laugh with whispered jest,
Guiding journeys east and west,
Maps of silk and compass free,
Tracing paths of fancy's sea.

Lighthouses of hope appear,
Casting beams through veils of clear,
Guiding hearts with steady glow,
Safe harbors where the wild winds blow.

Decks are strewn with flowers fair,
Each petal speaks a curious dare,
To leap beyond the anchor's claim,
And wander where the magic came.

Anchored whimsy, bound yet free,
A paradox of liberty,
Held in place by tethered dreams,
Floating on imagination's streams.

When Clouds Touch Earth

Mountains rise to kiss the sky,
Embracing clouds that drift and sigh,
In misty veils, the world transforms,
As heaven's dew to earth conforms.

Rains descend, soft kiss to ground,
Nurturing seeds with gentle sound,
Life awakens in the blend,
Where earth and sky begin to mend.

Fog wraps hills in silken threads,
Mysteries in shadows shed,
Whispers in the morning light,
Echoes of the stars' delight.

On twilight's edge, horizons blur,
Where dreams and reality concur,
In this dance of sky and land,
Fingers touch with grace, unplanned.

When clouds touch earth, a sacred pact,
Nature's bond in secret act,
Unity in realms that meet,
In every touch, the world complete.

Embodying Visions

Eyes that see beyond the night,
Visions clear in inner sight,
Dreams take shape within the mind,
Crafted thoughts of every kind.

Hands that mold the formless beams,
Turning echoes into themes,
Shaping wonders from within,
Birthing light where none has been.

Soul and spirit, canvas vast,
Every stroke a spell is cast,
Art and life in tangled weave,
Essence flows with each reprieve.

Colors blend in hallowed space,
Bearing truths we dare not face,
Yet in form, the visions dwell,
Harboring tales they yearn to tell.

Embodying visions, pure and true,
Reflections of a world askew,
In each image, heart and mind,
New horizons, redefined.

Substantial Echoes

Within the hollow canyons wide,
Where shadows dance and whispers bide,
The echoes, substantial, find their way,
Through twilight's dim and dawning gray.

Beneath the sky where stars align,
Forgotten realms in time enshrine,
The echoes call from distant yore,
To hearts that seek and spirits soar.

In caverns deep and forests still,
Where ancient dreams the nights fulfill,
The echoes speak in silent streams,
Of truths unseen and hidden dreams.

Through winds that weave the night anew,
In shadows mixed with morning's dew,
The echoes sing in voices old,
Of tales untold and promises bold.

From mountains high to valleys low,
The echoes in their whispers flow,
They bind the past to moments near,
In substantial echoes, crystal clear.

Breath in the Ethereal

Upon the breeze of twilight's call,
A whisper faint begins to fall,
A breath in realms ethereal light,
Where day meets dream in star-kissed night.

The veils of time in folds they drift,
With secrets bound in cosmic rift,
A breath that stirs the silent air,
In worlds unseen, beyond compare.

In moonlit glades where shadows play,
And night holds court in gentle sway,
The breath of ages softly sweeps,
Through ancient groves where memory sleeps.

Through clouds that float on silver wings,
In ever-changing, mystic rings,
The breath of time and space entwine,
In dances vast, both rare and fine.

Beneath the stars, in stillness deep,
Where dreams awake and sorrows sleep,
The breath in the ethereal glows,
A timeless song that always flows.

Material Dreams

In dreams where matter takes its form,
Through patterned storms and shadows warm,
The textures blend and weave the night,
In tapestries of dark and light.

The solid grasp of waking's hand,
In dreams dissolves to shifting sand,
Where fantasies in colors stream,
Through realms of structured, material dream.

In pillars tall and arches grand,
The night builds towers in shifting land,
Each stone a thought, each wall a plan,
In dream's domain, where visions span.

Through halls of mirrors, clear and bright,
Reflecting depths of boundless sight,
The dreams take shape and form anew,
In endless shades, both bold and true.

As dawn approaches, shadows flee,
The dreams of matter cease to be,
Yet echoes of their structures stay,
In waking thoughts of coming day.

Pulse of Dreamscapes

Beneath the veil where silence seeps,
The pulse of dreamscape softly creeps,
In rhythms pure and cadence true,
Through night's embrace and morning's hue.

The heartbeats in the dream fields vast,
Where echoes of the future past,
Resonate in spectral streams,
Throughout the land of fleeting dreams.

In twilight's glow and midnight's breath,
The pulse of life defying death,
Through luminous and shadowed trails,
It speaks in whispers, softly sails.

Through voids and realms of endless night,
The pulse maintains its steady light,
A beacon in the dreamer's flight,
Guiding through the boundless height.

When dawn invades with tender grace,
The pulse of dreamscapes finds its place,
In waking hearts and open skies,
In dreams' recall, where truth lies.

Whispers of Reality

In the quiet of the dawn, I hear it stir,
A whisper soft, a gentle purr.
Reality beckons, its call so clear,
In each fleeting shadow, it draws near.

Dreams may shatter, hopes may fray,
But truth remains, come what may.
In every sorrow, in every cheer,
Reality whispers, ever dear.

The sun may fade, the night may grow,
Yet truth's consistent, through ebb and flow.
In love, in loss, in every plea,
Reality whispers, quietly.

Life's a puzzle, each piece austere,
Yet its whisper, always here.
Reality speaks, so that we see,
In every shadow, a part of me.

Unmasked Reverie

In dreams we wander, vast and free,
A world unmasked, so wild, so true.
Reverie, unbounded, let us see,
The beauty in both me and you.

Each thought a petal, in a sea of bliss,
Unmasked and free, a gentle kiss.
Reverie's grasp, so light, so near,
Whispers softly, in our ear.

Beyond the clouds, beyond the veil,
Dreams take flight, to tell their tale.
A canvas blank, for all to see,
Unmasked reverie, wild and free.

Yet morning comes, with its stark light,
Dreams fade softly, into night.
But within our hearts, forever be,
The touch of reverie, wild and free.

Substance in the Shadows

In the calm of twilight, shadows play,
Forming shapes that dance and sway.
Substance hides in every fold,
Stories whispered, quietly told.

Night conceals, but does not erase,
Substance found in every place.
In shadows' depth, a truth unfolds,
In every quiet, the night holds.

Beauty thrives in shadows deep,
Secrets there, for eyes to keep.
Substance lies, not just in light,
In shadows too, in darkest night.

So seek within the quiet shade,
Where whispers form, where dreams are made.
Substance found, so gracefully,
In shadows deep, a part of thee.

Beyond Fleeting Thoughts

Thoughts arise, like morning's haze,
Fleeting moments, transient phase.
Yet beyond, a river flows,
Steady current, ever knows.

In the mind's vast, uncharted sea,
Thoughts drift by, wild and free.
But beneath, a depth profound,
Where truths eternal can be found.

Fleeting moments, here and gone,
Yet below, life's steady song.
In the depths, a constant beat,
Beyond the thoughts, a rhythmic feat.

So dive beneath, explore the deep,
Where endless truths forever sleep.
Beyond the fleeting, find your grace,
In deeper waters, true embrace.

Broken Reveries

In the midnight's gentle whisper,
nostalgia's shadow softly gleams,
fractured tales of yesteryear,
woven tightly in our dreams.

Stars cascade like tears so silent,
through the darkness, memories sail,
hope and sorrow intertwining,
in a long-forgotten trail.

Scattered pieces of what once was,
leave a tapestry so worn,
echoes of our fondest moments,
find their place midst hearts forlorn.

Musing on the paths we wandered,
phantoms dance within our eyes,
seeking solace in the fragments,
as the night absorbs our cries.

Where the daylight cannot touch us,
hide the broken reveries,
dreams as fragile as the starlight
sing their haunt in whispered pleas.

Under the Day's Stare

Beneath the firmament's azure,
the world unfolds her daily grace,
tiny moments, vast sensations,
marked by time's relentless pace.

Eyes that drink in morning's glory,
hear the symphony of dawn,
cast their gaze upon the wonders
till the evening light is gone.

Noonday sun, a blazing sentinel,
witnesses the heart's duress,
tells the stories etched in wrinkles,
weaves them into nature's dress.

Golden rays descend like whispers,
murmuring secrets in the breeze,
life unfolds in splendid verses,
underneath the ancient trees.

Beneath the sky's unyielding watch,
past and present merge in flare,
we live, we dream, we find ourselves,
underneath the day's bright stare.

Reality's Embrace

In the stillness of the morning,
truth awakens with the dawn,
shadows cast by gilded sunlight,
reveal the dreams that linger on.

Moments steeped in quiet wisdom,
wrap us in their tender fold,
whispering the age-old secrets,
stories both diverse and bold.

Every step is bound by meaning,
every breath a chance anew,
we embrace the starkest truths,
in the clarity of dew.

Masked illusions fall away,
surface shimmers bare and bright,
we uncover deeper essence,
in the gentle, honest light.

With each heartbeat, we discover,
deep within the present's trace,
the simple, profound beauty
of reality's embrace.

In the Realm of the Real

Where imagination falters,
truth begins its quiet reign,
nurturing the seeds of wisdom,
anchored in the fertile plain.

Vivid dreams may offer solace,
but within the real we find,
honest answers to our longings,
comfort of a grounded mind.

Mountains stand in steadfast silence,
rivers carve their ancient path,
life unfolds in measured cadence,
mirroring the earth's own math.

Facets of our fleeting moments,
solid as the time-worn rock,
show us we can build our futures,
from the bedrock and the chalk.

In the realm of stark truth's shadow,
where the heart and spirit heal,
we discover life's true meaning,
in the realm of the real.

Substantial Reflections

In mirrors deep, the thoughts arise
Where currents swirl, and truth belies
The whispers of a time once known
In shadows cast, in glimmers shown

Beneath the calm, the tempest spins
With quiet sighs, true tale begins
Lost memories, in silvered streams
Reflect a world of muted dreams

The ripples dance with quiet grace
Revealing secrets we embrace
Yet substance lies in what is seen
A transient dream of what has been

The moonlight graces surface clear
To highlight all we hold so dear
In each reflection, life unfolds
A tapestry of tales retold

And as we gaze, the past aligns
With future hopes, in gentle signs
Thus, in the depths, our souls connect
Through mirrored thoughts, we recollect

Beyond the Veil

Through mists of time, a whisper calls,
A realm unseen, where shadow falls.
In twilight's grace, where dreams ignite,
Beyond the veil, awaits the night.

In silence deep, where echoes fade,
A mystic dance, by moonlight swayed.
The unknown whispers, soft and frail,
Secrets held beyond the veil.

Stars align in patterns old,
Mysteries in the dark unfold.
A gateway hidden, thoughts prevail,
Journeys start beyond the veil.

With courage drawn from hearts so brave,
We seek the path, the hidden cave.
For answers lie where visions sail,
In realms of dreams beyond the veil.

To step through mists, to hear the call,
To dance with shadows, to rise and fall.
In twilight's arms, where we inhale,
Life's deeper truths, beyond the veil.

Dreams Anchored

In moonlit harbors, hearts find rest,
Dreams anchor in the silent quest.
Across the waves, where hopes entwine,
We drift on seas of time divine.

With sails unfurled, we chase the light,
Through tempests wild, through darkest night.
Stars above, our course align,
In dreams, our destinies combine.

Beneath the deep, where shadows play,
Oceans whisper what words can't say.
We anchor thoughts, in depths confined,
In dreams, our truest selves we find.

Voyages far, through mists and dreams,
Life's rivers flow in endless streams.
Anchored hearts in starlit brine,
In dreams, we cross the sacred line.

Upon this shore, where night meets day,
Our spirits, bold, in sunlight stay.
In realms of sleep, where hopes define,
We anchor dreams, forever mine.

In Between the Lines

Amidst the ink, where thoughts reside,
A world within, where secrets hide.
In words unspoken, truths unwind,
Magic dwells, in between the lines.

In pages old, with faded script,
Where shadows of the past have slipped.
Across the sands of countless times,
Mysteries lie in between the lines.

Silent whispers, between the prose,
A hidden path, where wisdom grows.
In letters carved, the soul defines,
Meanings change in between the lines.

The blank of space, a canvas wide,
For dreams and thoughts that will abide.
A story waits as night unwinds,
Life's essence found in between the lines.

As chapters turn and pages dance,
We find the threads of our advance.
In every pause, where heart aligns,
We live and breathe in between the lines.

Blurring the Abstract

In colors wild, where forms collide,
A fleeting glimpse, where truths reside.
With strokes and hues, perceptions pact,
We find our way, blurring the abstract.

A dance of light on canvas bare,
Where hidden dreams take shape and dare.
In chaos bright, our minds contract,
To see the world, blurring the abstract.

Echoes loud in silent space,
A vision forms, a different face.
With every line, new thoughts attract,
A deeper view, blurring the abstract.

Patterns bold in shadows cast,
A bridge between the future, past.
In every shape, meanings impact,
Life's essence wrought, blurring the abstract.

In twilight's glow, where edges meet,
The heart and soul find rhythm, beat.
In art's embrace, our fates enact,
Journeys begun, blurring the abstract.

www.ingramcontent.com/pod-product-compliance
Lightning Source LLC
LaVergne TN
LVHW020451070526
838199LV00063B/4917